To Daley
love
mum & dad

christmas '91

Twitchety is Daniel's rabbit,
and one day she leaves her hutch
to see the world...

Twitchety

Goes Hop-About

A Bedtime Story

by Barbara Lancaster
illustrated by Gill Guile

Copyright © 1989 by World International Publishing Limited.
All rights reserved throughout the world.
Published in Great Britain by World International Publishing Limited,
An Egmont Company, Egmont House, P.O. Box 111, Great Ducie Street, Manchester M60 3BL.
Printed in DDR. ISBN 0 7235 1264 7
Reprinted 1990

A CIP catalogue record for this book is available from the British Library

Twitchety, Daniel's white rabbit, was determined to see the world.

She sat in her wooden hutch day after day, twitching her nose and staring through the wire mesh at the green field beyond.

It was a cosy hutch, and while Twitchety sat inside enjoying her lettuce, she would dream of exploring the big, wide world.

Sometimes she thought she could hear other rabbits calling her from far away, and she would stamp her feet in reply.

Daniel looked after Twitchety very well. He gave her plenty to eat and drink, and he always kept her hutch clean.

But it wasn't enough for Twitchety. She wanted to see the big, wide world.

"See the world!" tittered Miffy Mouse. "How are *you* going to see the world, Twitchety? You're not even allowed to leave your hutch! Besides, it's very big. It goes right up to that huge green hedge at the end of the field."

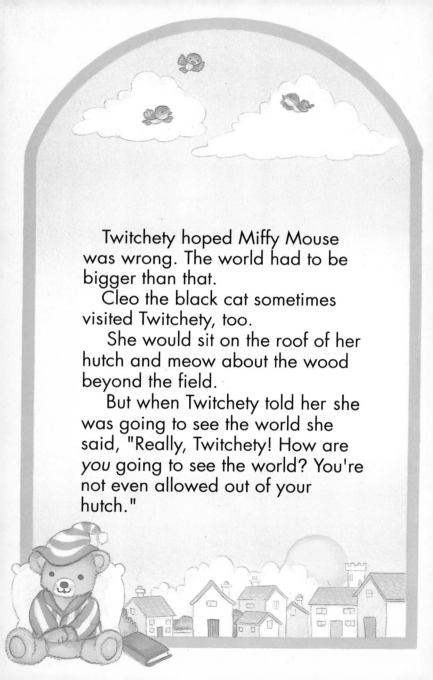

Twitchety hoped Miffy Mouse was wrong. The world had to be bigger than that.

Cleo the black cat sometimes visited Twitchety, too.

She would sit on the roof of her hutch and meow about the wood beyond the field.

But when Twitchety told her she was going to see the world she said, "Really, Twitchety! How are *you* going to see the world? You're not even allowed out of your hutch."

Twitchety went to the back of her hutch and sulked.

When Barny the owl called in on his way home, he said that the world was round. "It rolls away on the other side of the wood," he hooted.

This made Twitchety want to see the world even more.

"*You*, Twitchety?" said Barny. "How will you see the world? You're not even allowed out of your hutch." And with that, Barny flew off to his feathery bed.

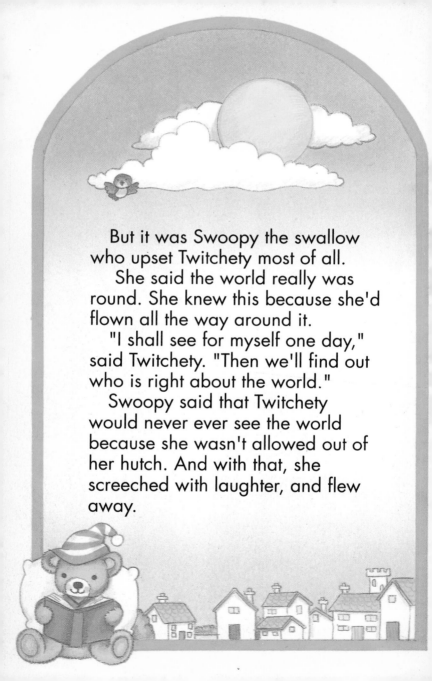

But it was Swoopy the swallow who upset Twitchety most of all.

She said the world really was round. She knew this because she'd flown all the way around it.

"I shall see for myself one day," said Twitchety. "Then we'll find out who is right about the world."

Swoopy said that Twitchety would never ever see the world because she wasn't allowed out of her hutch. And with that, she screeched with laughter, and flew away.

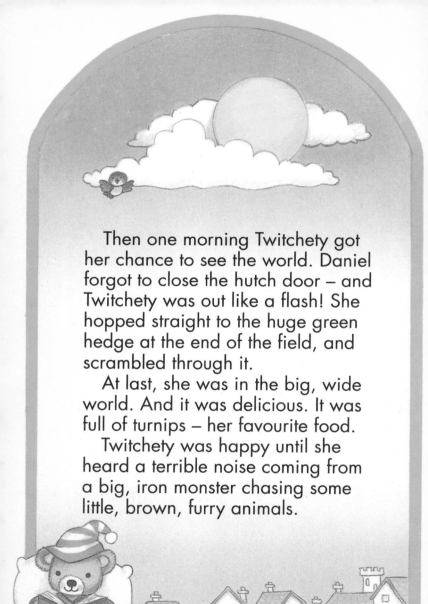

Then one morning Twitchety got her chance to see the world. Daniel forgot to close the hutch door – and Twitchety was out like a flash! She hopped straight to the huge green hedge at the end of the field, and scrambled through it.

At last, she was in the big, wide world. And it was delicious. It was full of turnips – her favourite food.

Twitchety was happy until she heard a terrible noise coming from a big, iron monster chasing some little, brown, furry animals.

The little animals had long ears and fluffy tails – just like Twitchety had.

"Run!" they shouted to Twitchety. "Run for your life!"

The iron monster was getting closer, and Twitchety started to run with the other animals.

She was surprised just how fast she could run, and in no time at all she was safe inside the wood at the end of the field.

The big machine rumbled past them and went away.

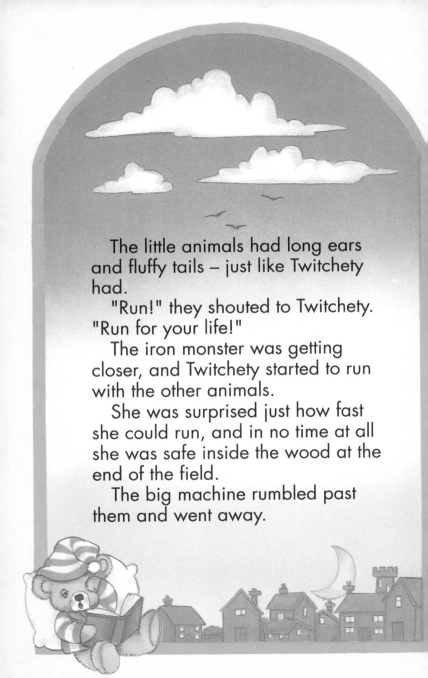

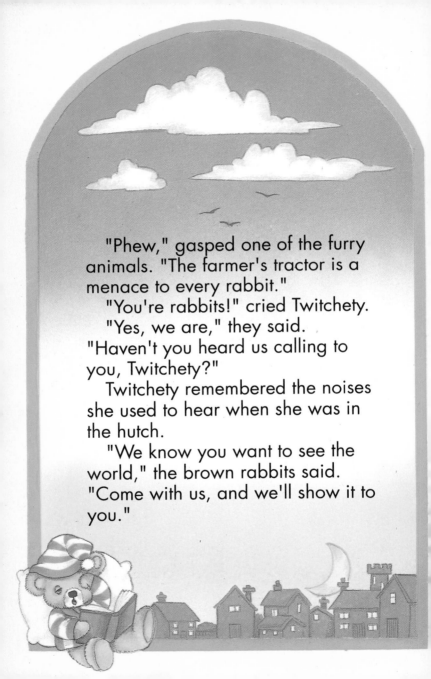

"Phew," gasped one of the furry animals. "The farmer's tractor is a menace to every rabbit."

"You're rabbits!" cried Twitchety.

"Yes, we are," they said. "Haven't you heard us calling to you, Twitchety?"

Twitchety remembered the noises she used to hear when she was in the hutch.

"We know you want to see the world," the brown rabbits said. "Come with us, and we'll show it to you."

Twitchety went with the rabbits as they hopped through the wood.

"Where are we going to?" she asked them.

"To our home on the common," said one of the wild rabbits. "I am called Brave One, and these are my brothers and sisters."

Twitchety followed them until they came to the common.

"Barny the owl was right!" said Twitchety. "The world really *does* roll away on the other side of the wood."

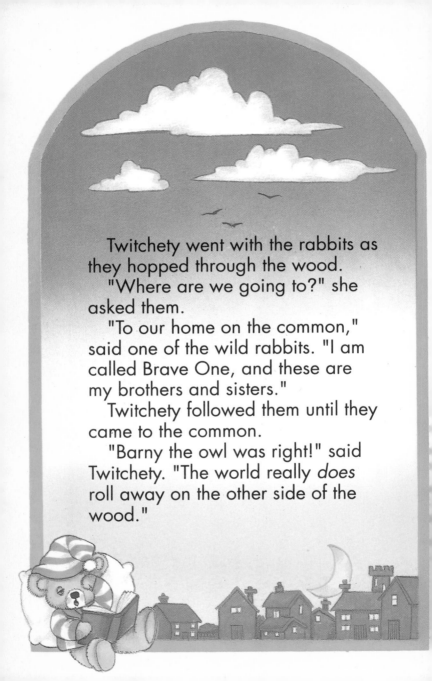

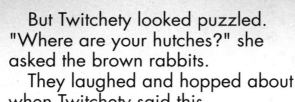

But Twitchety looked puzzled. "Where are your hutches?" she asked the brown rabbits.

They laughed and hopped about when Twitchety said this.

"We live in burrows in the earth," they said. Brave One took Twitchety and led her into one of the rabbit holes on the common.

Twitchety had never been inside a burrow before, and she soon decided she didn't like it.

It was hot and smelly, and not as comfortable as her own hutch.

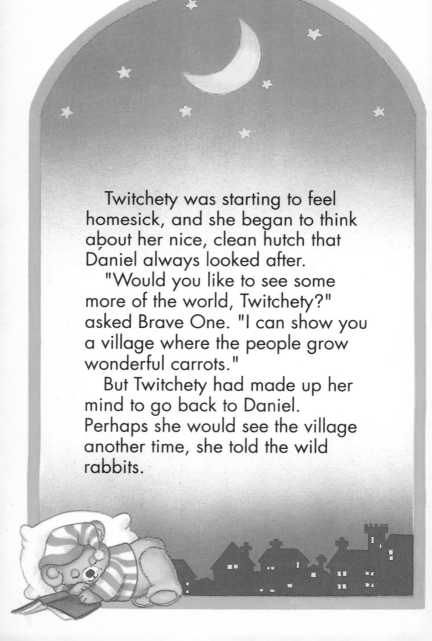

Twitchety was starting to feel homesick, and she began to think about her nice, clean hutch that Daniel always looked after.

"Would you like to see some more of the world, Twitchety?" asked Brave One. "I can show you a village where the people grow wonderful carrots."

But Twitchety had made up her mind to go back to Daniel. Perhaps she would see the village another time, she told the wild rabbits.

She thanked the brown rabbits
for showing her the world, and then
hopped back through the wood.

Daniel was overjoyed to see
Twitchety again. When she was
safely back inside her hutch,
Twitchety's friends came to see her.

"I've seen the world!" Twitchety
told Miffy, Cleo and Barny. "It's
much, *much* bigger than you think!"

From high up in the sky, Swoopy
swallow called out. "And one day
Twitchety you'll see the *whole*
world. It's a wonderful place!"